# FARM TO FORK
## WORKSHOP

## Making the Most of Local Foods

Megan Borgert-Spaniol

An imprint of Abdo Publishing
abdobooks.com

ABDOBOOKS.COM

Published by Abdo Publishing, a division of ABDO, PO Box 398166, Minneapolis, Minnesota 55439. Copyright © 2024 by Abdo Consulting Group, Inc. International copyrights reserved in all countries. No part of this book may be reproduced in any form without written permission from the publisher. Abdo & Daughters™ is a trademark and logo of Abdo Publishing.

Printed in the United States of America, North Mankato, Minnesota
052023
092023

Design: Aruna Rangarajan and Emily O'Malley, Mighty Media, Inc.
Production: Mighty Media, Inc.
Editor: Ruthie Van Oosbree
Recipes: Megan Borgert-Spaniol
Cover Photographs: Mighty Media, Inc.; Shutterstock Images
Interior Photographs: iStockphoto, pp. 4, 5 (bottom), 6 (top right, bottom), 11 (top right), 13 (middle right, top right), 18 (top, bottom right), 21 (left top, left bottom), 22, 23, 24 (top), 25 (top right, bottom right), 26, 28, 29 (top), 54 (bottom left, bottom right, middle), 58 (bottom left), 60, 61 (bottom); Mighty Media, Inc., pp. 30 (frittata, plate, pan), 32 (all), 33 (all), 34–35, 36 (food on plate), 38 (all), 39 (all), 40–41, 42 (squash), 44 (all), 45 (all), 46–47, 48 (stew), 50 (all), 51 (all), 52–53; Shutterstock Images, pp. 3, 5 (top), 6 (top left), 8 (all), 9, 10, 11 (bottom right, left all), 12 (all), 13 (bottom right, left all), 14, 15 (all), 16 (all), 17 (all), 18 (bottom left), 19 (all), 20 (all), 21 (right all), 24 (bottom four), 25 (top left, bottom left), 27 (all), 29 (bottom), 30 (background), 36 (background), 42 (background), 48 (background), 54 (top), 55, 56, 57, 58 (top, middle right, bottom right, middle left), 59, 61 (top)
Design Elements: Shutterstock Images

The following manufacturers/names appearing in this book are trademarks: Pyrex® and Wilton®

Library of Congress Control Number: 2022948834

PUBLISHER'S CATALOGING-IN-PUBLICATION DATA

Names: Borgert-Spaniol, Megan, author.
Title: Farm to fork workshop: making the most of local foods / by Megan Borgert-Spaniol
Other title: making the most of local foods
Description: Minneapolis, Minnesota : Abdo Publishing, 2024 | Series: Kitchen to career | Includes online resources and index.
Identifiers: ISBN 9781098291396 (lib. bdg.) | ISBN 9781098277857 (ebook)
Subjects: LCSH: Food--Juvenile literature. | Cooking--Juvenile literature. | Farm produce--Juvenile literature. | Subsistence farming--Juvenile literature. | Locally produced foods--Juvenile literature. | Food supply--Juvenile literature. | Occupations--Juvenile literature.
Classification: DDC 641.3--dc23

# CONTENTS

Making a Career in the Kitchen .............. 5

The Basics ................................................ 7

Getting Started ....................................... 11

- ◆ **Frittata with Peas & Asparagus** ........... 31
- ◆ **Salad with Grilled Chicken** ............... 37
- ◆ **Quinoa-Stuffed Squash** ........................... 43
- ◆ **Beef Stew** ....................... 49

Presentation & Beyond .......................... 54

Careers in the Kitchen ........................... 57

Glossary ................................................. 62

Online Resources ................................... 63

Index ...................................................... 64

# MAKING A CAREER IN THE KITCHEN

Are you fascinated by the way vegetables and meat caramelize in a hot pan? Do you love experimenting with recipes and making tweaks to improve them? Do you want to create meals inspired by farm-fresh products? If your answer to these questions is yes, you might be suited to a career as a cook or chef.

Becoming a cook or chef takes training and hard work. It takes dedication to craft, quality, and safety. But if you have a passion for cooking with fresh food, you may find that the dedication comes naturally and the hard work is worthwhile.

In this book, you'll learn about the farm-to-fork movement's history and about how the movement has influenced professional kitchens. You'll become familiar with basic ingredients, tools, and techniques used to create meals out of local and seasonal products. You'll practice using these ingredients, tools, and techniques in a few basic recipes. Then, you'll try following your own tastes and inspirations to modify recipes. Finally, you'll learn how you might turn your passion for cooking into a career.

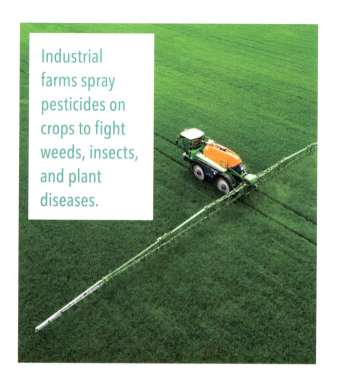

Industrial farms spray pesticides on crops to fight weeds, insects, and plant diseases.

In 2022, transporting food accounted for almost 20 percent of carbon emissions within the global food system.

The process of canning food was developed in 1809 for the French military. In the United States, canned goods first became commercially popular in the 1850s.

THE BASICS

# FROM THE FARM TO YOUR FORK

The phrase *farm to fork*, or *farm to table*, refers to food made with ingredients that are grown or produced locally. It also refers to a movement that prioritizes this kind of food. The movement came from a desire to return to a more sustainable way of life when people were more connected to their food sources.

Until the early 1900s, most Americans lived in rural areas. They relied on food products that were grown, raised, or produced on nearby land. But this soon changed. Industrialization led people to leave rural areas to work at factory jobs in cities. By the 1920s, most Americans had settled in urban areas.

As cities grew, small family farms gave way to large industrial ones. These large farms used new technologies to maximize food production. Meanwhile, innovations in food processing, storage, and transportation allowed foods to last longer and travel farther than ever before. Corn grown on a large farm in Iowa could be canned and shipped to grocery stores across the country. At the grocery stores, shoppers could purchase meat, produce, grains, and other foods without knowing where they came from.

Many Americans enjoyed the convenience of this food system. But in the 1960s and 1970s, some groups began to raise awareness about its faults. Animal advocates called attention to the poor conditions in which animals were raised on industrial farms. Environmental activists spoke out against the chemical pesticides and fertilizers used by industrial farms. They argued that these chemicals were bad for humans, wildlife, and the environment. Activists also called attention to the carbon emissions produced by transporting food from large farms across the country.

This heightened awareness about industrial farming practices led many consumers to be more mindful about where their food came from. For many, this meant supporting smaller

Industrial farms send vegetables and fruits to factories to be sorted, inspected, and packed before they are shipped to grocery stores.

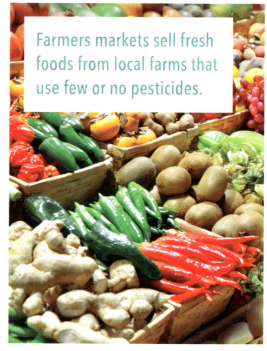
Farmers markets sell fresh foods from local farms that use few or no pesticides.

farms that considered the health and well-being of their animals, the environment, and the end consumer. It also meant supporting local farms in an effort to strengthen communities and decrease carbon emissions from transporting food long distances.

As individual consumers showed interest in supporting local producers, businesses began to do the same. Restaurants and other food establishments began to describe their offerings as "farm to table" or "farm to fork." This signaled to customers that the establishment sourced its ingredients from local farms and producers. Sourcing primarily local ingredients limited restaurant chefs and patrons to food that was seasonal, or recently harvested. But it also meant the ingredients were fresh, packed with nutrients, and full of flavor.

Today, individuals and businesses alike support the farm-to-fork movement by sourcing their food products from farmers markets, small local suppliers, or directly from farms. Some restaurants even maintain gardens where they grow their own produce. In the following pages, you'll learn about common ingredients, tools, and techniques for cooking with fresh, seasonal produce. Then you'll be ready to start your own farm-to-fork movement!

Produce at farmers markets is often less expensive than produce at grocery stores.

GETTING STARTED

# INGREDIENTS

Get familiar with some of the ingredients you'll see in this book's recipes.

### ALLIUMS

Garlic, onions, and shallots all belong to a group of plants known as alliums. They add varying degrees of sweetness and spiciness to dishes. These ingredients have more powerful flavors when eaten raw than when cooked.

### ASPARAGUS

Asparagus is a vegetable harvested in spring. An asparagus stalk has a tender tip at one end and a woody stem at the other. Green asparagus has a grassy, slightly bitter flavor. White asparagus has a somewhat milder flavor, while purple asparagus is sweeter and nuttier.

### BROTH

Broth is a seasoned liquid. Vegetable broth is made by simmering vegetables and herbs in water. Chicken and beef broths are made the same way, but with the addition of meat. Broth is used as a base for soups. It can also be used to cook grains, flavor sauces, and more.

### CHEESE

Cheese comes in hundreds of varieties, from soft and creamy to firm and salty. The recipes in this book use Gruyère, cheddar, and feta. Gruyère is creamy, nutty, and earthy. Cheddar is buttery and mild when young but develops a sharper flavor as it ages. Feta is crumbly, salty, and tangy.

### CITRUS

Lemon and lime juices bring acidity to dishes. They are often used to balance out rich or sweet flavors. These acids are also used in marinades because they help break down proteins in meat, making it more tender.

### SAUCES & CONDIMENTS

Mayonnaise provides a mild, creamy base for dressings, while Dijon mustard brings a sharper, tangier flavor. Soy and Worcestershire sauces both bring complex sweet and salty flavors to marinades, dressings, and more.

### HERBS & SPICES

Mint is an herb with a fresh, slightly sweet flavor that pairs well with ripe summer fruit. Cinnamon is a warm, woody spice that pairs well with squash, apples, and other sweet produce. Cumin and turmeric are earthy, peppery spices that deepen the flavor of soups and stews.

### KOSHER SALT & BLACK PEPPER

Salt is a mineral that brings its own flavor while also enhancing other flavors. The recipes in this book call for kosher salt, which is made of coarser grains than table salt. Black pepper comes from berries called peppercorns that are dried and ground up. It adds depth and spice to all kinds of dishes.

### LEAFY GREENS

Leafy greens are edible plant leaves. Some, like romaine lettuce, provide a mild flavor and refreshing crunch. Crunchy lettuces are often eaten raw in salads. Other greens, such as spinach, are more tender in texture and grassy in flavor. Spinach is commonly cooked with eggs or wilted in soups or stews.

### LENTILS

Lentils are legumes, a group of edible seeds that includes peas and beans. Lentils come in several varieties, including brown, green, and red. Rinse lentils before cooking to remove any dirt or debris.

### MEAT

A "cut" of meat refers to the part of the animal the meat comes from. Different cuts are suited to different dishes. Ham is a cut of pork from the hind thighs of a pig. Chicken breast is a cut of lean meat from the front of a chicken. Beef chuck comes from the shoulder of a cow. This firm cut requires long, slow cooking to become tender, making it perfect for stew.

### OIL & BUTTER

Oil and butter are fats that add richness to foods. These fats also allow meat, vegetables, and other foods to cook in hot pans without burning. Butter brings a sweet, nutty flavor to foods, but it burns at a lower temperature than oil. Olive oil has a bitter, grassy flavor and can withstand higher temperatures than butter. Vegetable oil has a neutral flavor and can withstand high heat.

### QUINOA

Though technically a seed, quinoa is often classified as a grain because of the way it is prepared and the nutrients it provides. Quinoa comes in a variety of colors, but the most common are red, white, and black.

### SQUASH

Although squash is cooked and eaten like a vegetable, it contains seeds and grows from flowers, making it a fruit. Zucchini is a type of squash harvested in the summer. Squashes harvested in the fall include acorn squash, butternut squash, and pumpkin.

### SWEETENERS

The products of cooking are often more savory than sweet. But cooks often use sweet ingredients to balance out salty flavors and make dishes more complex. Maple syrup, honey, and brown sugar all bring subtle sweetness to dressings, sauces, and marinades.

### TOMATO PASTE

Tomato paste is made of tomatoes that have been cooked down into a concentrated form. Just a little bit of the resulting paste adds deep flavor to sauces, stews, and more.

### VINEGARS

Cooks have a wide array of vinegars to choose from when they want to add a hint of acid to their dishes. While all vinegars are tart, their flavors differ from one variety to the next. Apple cider vinegar carries hints of the fruit it's made from. Balsamic vinegar is made from grapes, which lend a fruitier sweetness. Red wine vinegar is less sweet and more acidic than balsamic vinegar.

# KITCHEN TOOLS

Get familiar with some of the supplies you'll see in this book's recipes.

## BAKING SHEET

A baking sheet is a pan with a shallow rim around all four sides or no rim at all.

## BASTING BRUSH

A basting brush is a soft-bristled brush used to evenly coat pans or ingredients with oil. It is also used to spread glazes, marinades, and cooking juices over meat or vegetables. If you don't have a basting brush, you can do similar tasks with an unused paintbrush, a paper towel, or a silicone spatula.

## CAST IRON SKILLET

Cast iron skillets are heavy, durable pans that can withstand high temperatures and retain heat longer than pans made of aluminum or steel. This makes the pans good for techniques such as searing, stir-frying, or roasting. Cast iron is also oven safe, making it a popular choice for cooking frittatas, which start on the stove and finish in the oven.

## DUTCH OVEN

A Dutch oven is a heavy, durable pot used to cook food on the stove or in the oven. Most Dutch ovens are made of cast iron, allowing them to withstand high temperatures and retain heat. They are used for slow-cooking meats, roasting vegetables, and even baking bread!

### GRILL PAN

A grill pan is a type of skillet with raised lines crossing its surface. These lines create char lines, or grill marks, like those achieved by cooking on an outdoor grill grate. Char lines add flavor and texture to meat and vegetables.

### MEAT THERMOMETER

A meat thermometer measures the internal temperature of meat and fish. For an accurate reading, insert the thermometer into the thickest part of the meat.

### MUFFIN PAN

A muffin pan is a baking pan with indented cups that hold batter for baking. Muffin pans can also be used to make mini frittatas. Just be sure to fully grease each cup so the baked eggs come out cleanly.

## PARCHMENT PAPER

Parchment paper is a lightweight, heat-resistant, nonstick paper that helps prevent ingredients from burning or sticking to baking sheets. Parchment paper is only good for one or two uses. If you want to avoid paper waste, a silicone baking mat does the job of parchment paper but is washable and reusable.

## PLASTIC WRAP

Plastic wrap or cling wrap is a thin plastic film used to cover ingredients. The wrap creates an airtight seal that prevents the ingredients from drying out in the refrigerator. To avoid plastic waste, some cooks use reusable plastic bags or beeswax wrap instead of plastic wrap.

## WHISK

A whisk is used to thoroughly blend ingredients. When making a salad dressing, a whisk breaks down oil into tiny droplets that disperse throughout the rest of the liquid. When making a frittata, a whisk breaks the eggs down and helps incorporate them into the other ingredients.

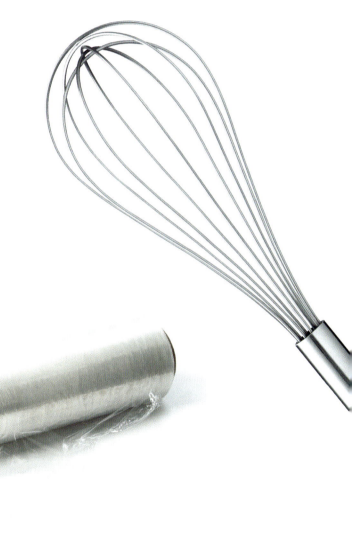

# TERMS & TECHNIQUES

Get familiar with some of the terms and techniques you'll see in this book's recipes.

## BRAISING

Braising is a cooking method that uses both dry and wet heat. First, meat is seared in fat to brown the outside. Then the meat is slowly cooked over low heat in a liquid such as broth. This long, slow cooking develops flavor and tenderizes the meat. Vegetables can also be braised.

## CHARRING

Char is a thin layer of dark, caramelized skin that forms where food touches a very hot surface. It adds flavor and texture to the cooked food. Charring goes a step beyond browning, but it stops short of burning. This can be a difficult balance to achieve! You can char food on a grill, in a stovetop pan, or in an oven.

## CHOPPING, DICING & MINCING

Chopping is a cutting technique that results in rough, uneven chunks of an ingredient.

Dicing is a more precise cutting technique that results in slightly smaller pieces of uniform size.

Mincing is cutting an ingredient into tiny pieces so its flavor spreads throughout a dish while its texture goes unnoticed.

## GRILLING

Grilling is cooking food at a high temperature while exposing it directly to the heat source. Grates create distinctive char lines on the surface of the food. Grilling is typically done outdoors with a charcoal, gas, or electric grill. But cooks can also use indoor grill appliances as well as stovetop grill pans to achieve a similar effect.

## MARINATING

Marinating is soaking meat, vegetables, or fish in a liquid solution, or marinade, before cooking. Marinades help flavor the food. They also usually contain acids, such as vinegar or lemon juice, that help tenderize the food.

### ROASTING VERSUS BAKING

Roasting and baking both involve cooking food with dry heat. However, they are not interchangeable methods. Roasting is cooking foods that already have a solid structure, such as vegetables or meat. Roasting requires high temperatures of 400°F or more to cook through foods and caramelize their exteriors to a crisp golden brown. Baking, on the other hand, is cooking foods that do not have a solid structure, such as batter, dough, or eggs. Baking requires temperatures around 375°F or lower.

### PREHEATING THE OVEN

Most foods benefit from an initial blast of heat to kick-start their caramelization. That's why it's a good idea to preheat your oven, or let it fully heat to the specified temperature, before you start charring or roasting.

## SAUTÉING

Sautéing is browning a food quickly over high heat. This is done in a shallow pan with a little bit of fat. Sautéing vegetables lets them retain some of their natural flavor and texture while still softening and browning them. You can also sauté thin, uniform cuts of tender meat and fish.

## SEARING

Searing is cooking the surface of a food over high heat with the goal of browning its exterior but not cooking it all the way through. This method is commonly used with thicker cuts of meat that finish cooking in the oven.

## SEASONING WITH SALT & PEPPER

Without salt and pepper, most dishes would taste bland. But too much salt and pepper will overpower the other flavors in the dish. Finding the right balance takes some trial and error. If a recipe says simply to season your ingredients, start with a generous pinch of salt and a smaller pinch of pepper. Try to taste your ingredients while cooking to make sure they are properly seasoned.

## SIMMERING VERSUS BOILING

If a recipe says to heat a liquid to a simmer, look for small bubbles that rise to the liquid's surface, causing gentle movement. If a recipe calls for boiling the liquid, look for many large bubbles rising at once, constantly disrupting the liquid's surface.

## KITCHEN PREP TIPS

> Have all your supplies out and ready before you begin. Gather all your ingredients on a tray or rimmed baking sheet. Then it's easy to slide everything out of the way if you need to make space.

> Wear an apron to protect your clothing. It will also serve as a hand towel.

# FINDING SEASONAL PRODUCTS

Farm-to-fork cooking starts with seasonal fruits and vegetables. The table below shows some of the produce that US farmers harvest during each season of the year. However, the seasonal produce in your area may vary depending on weather and growing conditions.

| Spring | Summer | Fall | Winter |
| --- | --- | --- | --- |
| asparagus | avocados | apples | carrots |
| lemon | bell peppers | brussels sprouts | celery |
| mushrooms | berries | cabbage | citrus fruits |
| peas | cherries | cauliflower | leeks |
| radishes | corn | cranberries | onions |
| rhubarb | mangoes | kale | pears |
| spinach | tomatoes | onions | potatoes |
| Swiss chard | watermelon | squash | sweet potatoes |

## BEYOND PRODUCE

Fruits and vegetables aren't the only seasonal products. Beef is best in the late fall and early winter, after cows have grazed on sweet grass. Eggs and chickens are naturally abundant during spring and summer. Beekeepers harvest honey around the end of summer, and maple syrup producers collect sap in late winter and early spring. All these products can be found year-round at grocery stores. But cooks following a farm-to-fork model try to honor the natural seasons of each product.

# FOOD PREP TIPS & TRICKS

Produce tastes best when it is farm fresh. But it also takes a bit of time and skill to prepare the produce so it can shine. Here are a few tips and tricks for preparing the produce in this book.

Make sure the blade of your knife is sharp. A dull blade is more dangerous than a sharp one because it requires more force to cut through produce.

There are various techniques for cutting a watermelon into cubes. One is to slice off the ends so the watermelon can sit on a solid base. Carefully slice off the rind in sections from the top end of the watermelon to the bottom. Then cut the fruit into quarter wedges. Cut the wedges into strips and then cubes.

To cube a butternut squash, start by slicing off the ends and laying the squash on its side. Then use a vegetable peeler to remove the skin. Cut the peeled squash in half down its length and scoop out the seeds with a spoon. Then slice and cube the squash.

Cut an avocado in half along its length by running your knife around the pit in the middle of the fruit. Pull the two halves apart. Then tap the blade of the knife into the pit and pull the pit out of the avocado.

After washing fresh berries, fully dry them in single layer on a towel. This prevents excess moisture from clinging to the berries and making your dish watery.

To avoid a soggy salad, thoroughly dry lettuce after washing it. A salad spinner is a great tool for this. If you don't have a spinner, lay the lettuce on a towel in a single layer and let it air-dry.

The tough, woody end of an asparagus stalk should be removed before cooking the asparagus. Hold one end of the asparagus in each hand and gently bend the stalk until the woody end snaps off.

## FOOD SAFETY TIPS

- Make sure your prep surface is clean and dry. Wash your hands with soap and water before and after you handle ingredients.
- Don't eat uncooked eggs or meat. Thoroughly wash your hands and all surfaces after handling raw meat.
- Place any leftover ingredients into containers with lids. Use tape and markers to label each container with the ingredient and the date. Keep the containers somewhere you will easily see them so you don't forget about them.

# CREATING IN THE KITCHEN

Recipes are great for learning how to cook. But as you get comfortable following recipes, you might start imagining ways to improve them.

Maybe you want to add mushrooms or kale to a soup recipe you love. Or maybe you decide to sweeten your salad dressing with honey from a local farm.

This book includes four formal seasonal recipes meant to help you practice working with different ingredients and techniques. Following each formal recipe is an informal companion. These companion recipes are less structured and provide fewer details. This leaves room for you, the cook, to follow your own tastes and preferences. If an informal recipe doesn't suit your taste, check out the accompanying "Experiment!" sidebar for additional ideas. With some thought and creativity, you can make any recipe your own way.

## CONVERSION CHART

| Standard | Metric |
|---|---|
| ¼ teaspoon | 1.25 mL |
| ½ teaspoon | 2.5 mL |
| 1 teaspoon | 5 mL |
| 1 tablespoon | 15 mL |
| ¼ cup | 60 mL |
| ⅓ cup | 80 mL |
| ½ cup | 125 mL |
| ⅔ cup | 160 mL |
| ¾ cup | 175 mL |
| 1 cup | 240 mL |
| 165°F | 74°C |
| 325°F | 160°C |
| 350°F | 180°C |
| 375°F | 190°C |
| 400°F | 200°C |

# RULES TO REMEMBER

As you start putting your own twist on recipes, keep these guiding principles in mind.

**Master the basics first.** Start out following recipes exactly as they are written. You'll better understand how ingredients combine and behave, and this knowledge will inform your decisions as you go off-book.

**Every cook has their own methods.** You might see another cook thicken soup with cornstarch while you use flour. Or, a cook may cut up a squash differently from how you learned. This doesn't mean you have to change your ingredients or techniques. If you can, ask a cook why their methods work for them. Test the methods yourself and decide what works best for you!

**Experiments don't always go to plan.** Don't be crushed if you overcooked your chicken breast or under-salted your stew. If the results are still edible, don't let them go to waste! Instead, think of how you can make them tastier. If your chicken is dry, top it with a sauce or add it to a soup. If your stew tastes bland, stir in some grated Parmesan, sour cream, or fresh herbs.

**Cooking is often called an art, not a science.** A recipe won't be ruined by an extra clove of garlic or a missed teaspoon of lime juice. Cooks are always tweaking and testing their recipes. Enjoy the process and take pride in the results.

*Make this!*

## SPRING
# FRITTATA WITH PEAS & ASPARAGUS

A frittata is an Italian dish of eggs whipped with milk or cream and cooked with cheese, meat, or vegetables. This frittata features bright green springtime produce. It's the perfect dish for a sunny weekend brunch!

## INGREDIENTS

- 8 eggs
- ½ cup milk
- 1 cup grated Gruyère
- 10 asparagus spears
- 1 tablespoon olive oil
- 1 tablespoon butter
- 1 shallot, diced
- 1 clove garlic, minced
- 1 cup shelled peas
- kosher salt & pepper

## SUPPLIES

- oven
- mixing bowl
- measuring cups and spoons
- cheese grater
- whisk
- knife and cutting board
- cast iron skillet
- stove
- mixing spoon

**1**

Preheat the oven to 375°F. In a medium bowl, whisk together the eggs, milk, and ½ cup of the grated Gruyère. Set the bowl aside.

**2**

Snap off and discard the woody ends of the asparagus spears. Chop the rest of the spears.

**3** Heat the olive oil and butter in the cast iron skillet over medium heat. Add the shallot, garlic, asparagus, and peas to the skillet and stir.

**4**

Season the vegetables with salt. Cook for about five minutes, stirring occasionally, until the vegetables are tender.

**5**

Season the egg mixture with salt and pepper. Then pour the mixture over the vegetables.

**6**

Cook the eggs without stirring for three to five minutes or until the eggs are set around the edges.

**7** Sprinkle the remaining Gruyère over the frittata. Transfer the skillet to the oven and bake for about 15 minutes or until the frittata is golden brown. Let the frittata cool slightly before serving.

### MAKE IT YOUR WAY

# SPINACH, HAM & CHEESE
# MINI FRITTATAS

Make bite-size frittatas using a muffin pan! And while you're at it, why not try new fillings?

In an oiled skillet, cook chopped shallot and garlic with 2 cups fresh spinach, stirring frequently. Season with salt and pepper.

### EXPERIMENT!
Play with different ingredient combinations, such as tomato and basil, corn and zucchini, or onions and peppers. Experiment with baking dishes of different shapes and sizes, which will alter the thickness of your frittatas.

Divide the cooked spinach among the greased cups of a muffin pan. Sprinkle cubed ham and shredded cheese over the spinach. Then pour egg mixture into each muffin cup, filling to the top.

Bake the mini frittatas at 375°F for about 15 minutes or until the eggs are set and golden.

MAKE THIS!

# SUMMER SALAD WITH GRILLED CHICKEN

Summer produce bursts with color and flavor. Char it on the grill to deepen the flavors. Then toss everything into a bowl with grilled chicken and romaine lettuce for the ultimate summertime salad!

## INGREDIENTS

**MARINATED CHICKEN:**
- ½ tablespoon olive oil
- 1 teaspoon soy sauce
- 1 teaspoon Worcestershire sauce
- 1 teaspoon lemon juice
- 1 teaspoon balsamic vinegar
- ½ tablespoon brown sugar
- 1 clove garlic, minced
- kosher salt & pepper
- 1 boneless, skinless chicken breast
- vegetable oil for brushing

**SALAD:**
- vegetable oil for brushing
- 1 red bell pepper
- 1 mango
- 2 ears of corn
- 1 bunch romaine lettuce
- 1 avocado
- feta for sprinkling

**DRESSING:**
- 3 tablespoons olive oil
- 1 tablespoon balsamic vinegar
- kosher salt & pepper

## SUPPLIES

- mixing bowls
- whisk
- measuring cups and spoons
- plastic wrap
- refrigerator
- tongs
- knife and cutting board
- grill pan (or outdoor grill)
- stove
- basting brush
- spatula
- meat thermometer
- plate
- serving dish

**1** In a small mixing bowl, whisk together the olive oil, soy sauce, Worcestershire sauce, lemon juice, balsamic vinegar, brown sugar, and garlic. Season the mixture with salt and pepper.

**2** Place the chicken breast in the bowl and season it with salt and pepper. Cover the bowl with plastic wrap and place it in the refrigerator for an hour. Flip the chicken with tongs halfway through.

**3** Heat the grill pan over high heat for two to three minutes. Use a basting brush to coat the pan with vegetable oil.

**4** Cut the red pepper into quarters and remove the stem and any white flesh. Place the quarters on the grill pan, insides facing down. After about eight minutes, flip them with tongs. Cook for another eight minutes, or until the peppers are grilled to your liking.

**5** Set aside the grilled red peppers. Slice off the fleshy parts of the mango, avoiding the pit. Use a knife to score each fleshy piece of the mango into cubes, but don't slice through the peel.

Brush the mango flesh with oil. Place the mango flesh-side down on the grill pan. Grill the mango for about three minutes or until you see char marks on the flesh.

38

**7**

Set aside the grilled mango. Cut the kernels off the ears of corn and spread them out in a single layer in the grill pan. Use a spatula to stir the kernels as they cook for about four minutes. They should appear golden and slightly charred.

**8** Transfer the corn to a bowl. Heat the grill pan over high heat for two minutes. Then brush the pan with oil and lower the heat to medium high.

**9**

Place the marinated chicken breast on the pan and cook without turning for six to eight minutes. Then flip the chicken and cook the other side for another six to eight minutes.

Use the thermometer to check that the chicken has an internal temperature of at least 165°F.

**10**

While the cooked chicken rests on a plate, begin assembling the salad. Chop the lettuce and transfer it to the large serving dish. Slice the grilled chicken and red pepper and add them to the dish along with the corn.

**11** Invert the mango peel so the scored cubes fall into the salad. As with the mango, cube the avocado in the peel and invert it over the salad.

**12** Whisk together the dressing ingredients in a small bowl. Add the dressing and sprinkle the feta over the salad before serving.

39

| MAKE IT YOUR WAY |

# WATERMELON SALAD

Toss fresh fruits with a honey-citrus dressing for a refreshing side salad!

Chop a watermelon into cubes. Slice strawberries into halves or quarters. Add everything to a serving bowl along with blueberries.

## EXPERIMENT!

Add or swap in cherries, blackberries, or other fruits. Try using lemon juice instead of lime juice or basil instead of mint. Top the salad with pistachios or crumbly cheese for added flavor and texture!

Whisk together a dressing of equal parts honey and lime juice, along with some lime zest and a pinch of salt. Chop some mint leaves into thin ribbons.

Top the salad with the mint and dressing.

[ MAKE THIS! ]

## FALL
# QUINOA-STUFFED SQUASH

For many cooks, fall is squash season. In this recipe, acorn squash halves are filled with apples, nuts, and other autumn flavors for the perfect harvest meal.

## INGREDIENTS

- 1 acorn squash
- 1 tablespoon olive oil
- kosher salt & pepper
- ¼ cup quinoa
- ½ cup vegetable broth
- ½ cup diced yellow onion
- ½ cup diced apple
- 2 cloves garlic, minced
- ¼ cup chopped walnuts

DRESSING:
- 1 tablespoon olive oil
- ½ tablespoon maple syrup
- ½ tablespoon apple cider vinegar
- 1 teaspoon Dijon mustard
- ¼ teaspoon cinnamon
- kosher salt & pepper

## SUPPLIES

- oven
- knife and cutting board
- spoon
- basting brush
- measuring cups and spoons
- parchment paper
- baking sheet
- small pot with cover
- stove
- mixing spoon
- large pan
- mixing bowl
- whisk

**1**

Preheat the oven to 400°F. Cut the acorn squash in half and scoop out the seeds. Brush the halves with ½ tablespoon olive oil and season with salt and pepper. Place the halves cut-side down on a parchment-lined baking sheet and roast for about 35 minutes.

**2**

Pour the quinoa and vegetable broth into a small pot. Cover the pot and place it over medium-high heat until the broth starts to boil. Turn the heat down to low to bring the broth to a simmer. Cook the quinoa for about 15 minutes or until all the liquid has cooked off. Stir the cooked quinoa and set aside.

**3**

While the quinoa cooks, heat ½ tablespoon olive oil in a pan over medium-high heat. Add the onion, apple, and garlic, and turn the heat down to medium. Sauté the ingredients for five to seven minutes or until they are slightly tender and browned. Season with salt and pepper.

**4**

In the mixing bowl, whisk together the olive oil, maple syrup, apple cider vinegar, Dijon mustard, cinnamon, salt, and pepper.

**5**

Add the cooked quinoa, sautéed ingredients, and walnuts to the bowl of dressing and stir everything together.

**6**

Divide the quinoa mixture between the two roasted squash halves. Put the filled squash back into the oven for 10 to 15 minutes or until the quinoa is slightly crispy.

[ MAKE IT YOUR WAY ]

# SQUASH TACOS

Fill corn tortillas with squash, quinoa, and cabbage slaw for colorful harvest tacos!

Peel and cube a butternut squash. Toss it in olive oil and season with salt and pepper. Then roast the squash at 400°F for about 20 minutes.

### EXPERIMENT!

Try using a different squash variety, such as delicata or acorn. Add black beans to the mix, or swap out the quinoa for spicy chorizo. If you'd rather skip the cabbage slaw, toss chopped kale in oil and let it roast with the squash for the last five minutes.

Cook the quinoa in vegetable broth or water. Meanwhile, whisk together a dressing of three parts mayonnaise to one part apple cider vinegar. Season with salt and pepper. Then toss shredded red cabbage and sliced onion in the dressing to make a slaw.

Heat corn tortillas in a hot pan. Fill each tortilla with cooked quinoa, roasted squash, and cabbage slaw.

MAKE THIS!

# WINTER BEEF STEW

This warm and nourishing stew features braised beef and two cold-weather staples: carrots and potatoes.

## INGREDIENTS

- 1 pound (½ kg) boneless beef chuck, cut into 1-inch (2.5 cm) chunks
- kosher salt & pepper
- 1½ tablespoons olive oil
- ½ yellow onion, chopped
- 3 cloves garlic, minced
- ⅓ cup red wine vinegar
- 3 tablespoons tomato paste
- 1 tablespoon Worcestershire sauce
- 2 cups beef broth
- 1 cup water
- 2–3 large carrots, peeled and cut into ¾-inch (1.9 cm) chunks
- 2–3 large yellow potatoes, cut into 1-inch (2.5 cm) chunks

## SUPPLIES

- knife and cutting board
- vegetable peeler
- paper towel
- measuring cups and spoons
- Dutch oven or similar oven-safe pot with cover
- stove
- tongs
- plate
- mixing spoon
- oven

1. Use a paper towel to pat the beef chunks dry. Then season all sides of the beef chunks with salt and pepper.

2. Heat 1 tablespoon olive oil in the Dutch oven over medium-high heat. Sear the beef in batches so it can cook in a single layer. Use tongs to turn the chunks until all sides are browned. Then transfer the seared meat to a plate.

3. Heat ½ tablespoon olive oil in the Dutch oven. Add the onions and garlic. Cook, stirring occasionally, for about three minutes or until the onions are slightly browned.

4. Stir the red wine vinegar, tomato paste, and Worcestershire sauce into the Dutch oven and cook for about 30 seconds.

Pour the beef broth and water into the pot. Stir the mixture and cover the Dutch oven.

**6** Preheat the oven to 325°F. When the broth starts to boil, add the seared beef back into the Dutch oven. Cover the Dutch oven again and transfer it to the oven. Braise the beef for about two hours.

Take the Dutch oven out of the oven and season the broth with salt. Add the carrots and potatoes. Put the covered Dutch oven back into the oven for about an hour, or until the vegetables are tender.

**8** Season the stew as desired before serving.

MAKE IT YOUR WAY

# CARROT, POTATO & LENTIL SOUP

Make a vegetarian alternative to beef stew using hearty brown lentils!

Cook chopped onion and garlic in olive oil until they are slightly browned. Season with salt and pepper. Then add tomato paste, a teaspoon each of cumin and turmeric, and ½ cup lentils. Cook while stirring for 30 seconds.

## EXPERIMENT!
Use sweet potato instead of yellow potato. Test out different spices, such as coriander and ginger, or herbs, such as oregano and thyme. Try adding greens, such as kale or spinach, as the soup finishes cooking.

Add chopped carrots and potatoes to the pot along with vegetable broth and water. Season with salt.

Bring the soup to a boil, then turn down the heat. Let the soup simmer for about 20 minutes or until the vegetables and lentils are tender.

# PRESENTATION & BEYOND

Your dish is complete, but you're not done yet! It's time to think about how to display and serve your creation. Just as important is how you preserve any leftovers.

A frittata in a cast iron skillet makes for a beautiful centerpiece. Display it whole, then slice it and serve your guests at the table.

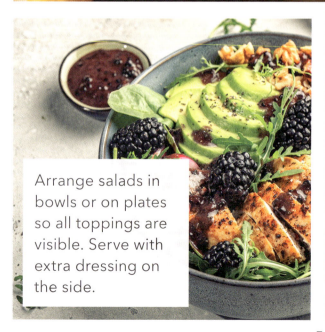

Arrange salads in bowls or on plates so all toppings are visible. Serve with extra dressing on the side.

Serve stews with a garnish of fresh herbs and a side of crusty bread. The bread is perfect for soaking up the rich broth!

Serve stuffed squash halves open-faced with a garnish of herbs, seeds, or cheese. If you cut off the squash tops, roast them and place them back on the squashes like top hats!

## STORING LEFTOVERS

> Refrigerate leftover frittata in an airtight container for three to four days. To preserve it longer, wrap individual portions in plastic and freeze them in an airtight bag or container.

> A lettuce salad that has been tossed with dressing will wilt quickly. If you can, refrigerate all elements of your salad separately, especially the dressing. Then combine the ingredients at mealtime.

> If you want to store leftover stuffed squash for more than a few days, freeze it in an airtight container. Reheat frozen squash in a 350°F oven.

> Refrigerate leftover stew in containers with tight-fitting lids. If you choose to freeze the stew, leave about ½ inch (1.3 cm) of space at the top of each container, as the stew will expand as it freezes.

## SPECIAL CONSIDERATIONS

> Store unused lettuce in an airtight container lined with paper towels to absorb extra moisture that can make the lettuce soggy. Avoid tightly packing the lettuce, as this leads to rotting.

> Refrigerate foods within two hours, even hot foods. Divide hot foods like stew into small containers to help them cool quickly.

CAREERS IN THE KITCHEN

# BECOMING A CHEF

As you gain more knowledge and experience cooking seasonal dishes, you might decide to turn your hobby into a living. There are many ways to pursue a career in cooking!

### FORMAL SCHOOLING
Culinary and technical schools offer culinary arts programs that last anywhere from a few months to several years. These programs offer instruction in food science, knife skills, flavor development, and more. They also prepare students for work in professional kitchens.

### APPRENTICESHIP
Professional kitchens offer hands-on experience through apprenticeships and internships. These positions are often part-time and unpaid.

### ON-THE-JOB TRAINING
Some establishments hire employees with no formal training. New cooks learn from experienced coworkers. Often, a new cook's wages increase as they gain more experience.

### SELF-TEACHING
Many professional chefs learned much of what they know by reading cookbooks, watching others, and practicing in their own kitchens.

# COOKS & CHEFS AT WORK

As a farm-to-fork cook or chef, you can work in a variety of establishments. Read about a few of them below. Think about which suit you best and why.

## RESTAURANTS

A restaurant chef is in charge of creating the menu and managing the kitchen staff. Cooks follow a chef's orders and recipes to prepare the dishes on the menu.

## FOOD CO-OPS

A food co-op is a grocery store owned by the people who shop there. Co-ops establish relationships with nearby farms and producers in an effort to sell local, seasonal products. Many co-ops employ chefs or cooks to prepare fresh dishes for shoppers to purchase.

## PRIVATE KITCHENS

Some chefs cook for clients in the clients' homes. These chefs might work full-time in one home, planning and cooking every meal for the people who live there. Chefs can also do personal cooking for several different clients on a less regular basis, such as once a week or month.

## CATERING COMPANIES

Catering companies provide food services for large gatherings, such as weddings or corporate events. Catering chefs plan the menus for these events and oversee food preparation by the cooks.

Depending on where you work, cooking professionally can be drastically different from home cooking. As you think about cooking for a living, consider some of the tools, rules, and schedules of a professional chef.

## TOOLS

The tools of a professional kitchen are built to cook large quantities of food over several hours. Some restaurants need 10-burner stovetops to accommodate many pots and pans at once. Commercial deep fryers hold vats of hot oil, and large griddles can cook more than 20 burgers at a time. Professional kitchens might also have walk-in refrigerators, freezers, and pantries to store all the food needed for restaurant service.

## RULES

Cooks and chefs must uphold cleanliness and food safety standards. These standards range from wearing a uniform and keeping hair pulled back to properly storing ingredients and thoroughly cleaning equipment after use. Kitchen staff must also follow rules to protect themselves and others from common kitchen hazards, such as hot pans and wet floors.

## SCHEDULES

The schedule of a cook or chef depends in part on where they work. Restaurant kitchen staff often work 12 hours a day and six or seven days a week. Catering professionals may work most nights and weekends. Private chefs work around the schedules of their clients. No matter where they work, chefs and cooks can expect to put in long hours on their feet.

# DO WHAT YOU LOVE!

Being a cook or chef requires long shifts, hard physical work, and attention to rules and standards. These requirements can be difficult for home cooks to adjust to. But many professionals find the rewards of their work outweigh the difficulties. These rewards include being creative, getting exercise, and learning new skills.

Maybe your goal is to manage a high-volume kitchen. Maybe you have your sights set on opening a small farm-to-table operation. Or perhaps you are happy to keep cooking as a hobby but not as a career. As long as you do what you love, you'll love what you do.

# GLOSSARY

**advocate**—a person who defends or supports a cause.

**appliance**—a household or office device operated by gas or electric power. Common kitchen appliances include stoves, refrigerators, and dishwashers.

**apprenticeship**—an arrangement in which a person learns a trade or a craft from a skilled worker.

**caramelize**—to cook a food until the sugars in it brown, creating a sweet, nutty flavor. This process is called caramelization.

**culinary**—having to do with the kitchen or cooking.

**disperse**—to spread something evenly throughout something else.

**edible**—safe to eat.

**enhance**—to increase or make better.

**establishment**—a place or organization where people do business.

**incorporate**—to include or work into.

**industrial**—of or having to do with factories and making things in large quantities. Industrialization is the transition to an industrial economy.

**innovation**—a new idea, method, or device.

**internship**—a program that allows a student or graduate to gain guided practical experience in a professional field.

**pesticide**—a substance used to destroy pests.

**silicone**—a nontoxic substance made of silicon and oxygen atoms. It can take a rubber-like form, which is heat-resistant and used in many cooking and baking tools.

**soggy**—heavy and overly moist.

**sustainable**—relating to a method of using a resource so that the resource is not used up or damaged.

**technique**—a method or style in which something is done.

**tenderize**—to make softer or easier to cut and chew.

# ONLINE RESOURCES

To learn more about careers in farm-to-fork cooking, please visit **abdobooklinks.com** or scan this QR code. These links are routinely monitored and updated to provide the most current information available.

# INDEX

activists, 7
alliums, 11, 23, 29, 31-32, 34, 37-38, 43-44, 47, 49-50, 52
America, 7

basting brushes, 15, 37-39, 43-44
boiling, 21, 44, 51, 53
bowls, 31-32, 37-39, 40, 43, 45, 54
braising, 18, 49, 51
broth, 11, 18, 43-44, 47, 49, 51, 53-54
brown sugar, 13, 37-38

carbon emissions, 7-8
careers, 5, 8, 57-59, 61
cast iron skillets, 15, 31-33, 37, 54
catering, 58-59
charring, 16, 18-19, 37-39
cheese, 11, 29, 31-35, 37, 39-40, 55
citrus, 11, 19, 23, 29, 37-38, 40-41
color, 11-13, 18, 20-21, 31, 33, 35, 37-39, 44, 46, 50, 52
condiments, 12, 37-38, 43, 45, 47, 49-50
consumers, 7-8

dressing, 12-13, 17, 27, 37, 39-41, 43, 45, 47, 54-55
drying, 17, 25, 50
Dutch ovens, 15, 49-51

eggs, 12, 16-17, 20, 23, 25, 31-33, 35

farms, 5, 7-8, 23-24, 27, 58, 61
fats, 13, 15, 17-18, 21, 31-32, 34, 37-39, 43-46, 49-50, 52, 59
flavor, 8, 11-13, 16, 18-19, 21, 23-24, 27, 29, 37, 40, 43, 57
fruit, 11-13, 23-25, 29, 34, 37-41, 43-47, 55

graters, 29, 31-32
grocery stores, 7, 23, 58

herbs, 11-12, 29, 34, 40-41, 52, 54-55

industrialization, 7
Iowa, 7

juice, 11, 15, 19, 29, 37-38, 40-41

kitchens, 5, 57-59, 61
knives, 19, 24, 29, 31-32, 37-39, 43-44, 46, 49, 55, 57

lentils, 12, 23, 31-32, 46, 52-53

maple syrup, 13, 23, 43, 45
marinades, 11-13, 15, 19, 37-39
measuring, 16, 21, 27, 29, 31-32, 34, 37, 43-44, 49-50
meat, 5, 7, 11-13, 15-16, 18-21, 23, 25, 29, 31, 37-39, 49-52

nuts, 40, 43, 45

ovens, 15, 18, 20-21, 27, 31-33, 35, 43-46, 49, 51, 55

pans, 5, 13, 15-19, 21, 34-35, 37-39, 43-44, 47, 59
parchment paper, 17, 43-44
peelers, 24, 46, 49
pesticides, 7
plastic wrap, 17, 37-38, 55
pots, 15, 43-44, 49-51, 53, 59
preparation, 13, 19-20, 22, 24-25, 32, 38, 40, 44, 46, 50, 58
preservation, 7, 54-55

quinoa, 13, 43-47

recipes
  beef stew, 49-51
  carrot, potato & lentil soup, 52-53
  frittata with peas & asparagus, 31-33
  quinoa-stuffed squash, 43-45
  salad with grilled chicken, 37-39
  spinach, ham & cheese mini frittatas, 34-35
  squash tacos, 46-47
  watermelon salad, 40-41
refrigerators, 17, 37-38, 55, 59
restaurants, 8, 58-59
roasting, 15, 20, 44-47, 55

safety, 5, 7-8, 15, 22, 24-25, 59
salad, 12, 17, 25, 27, 37, 39-41, 54-55
sauces, 11-13, 29, 37-38, 49-50
sautéing, 21, 44-45
searing, 15, 18, 21, 50-51
seasons, 5, 8, 23, 27, 43, 57-58
simmering, 11, 21, 44, 53
soup, 11-12, 27, 29, 52-53
spatulas, 15, 37, 39,
spices, 12, 21, 31, 33-34, 37-38, 43-47, 49, 50, 52
stew, 12-13, 29, 49, 51-52, 54-55
stoves, 15, 18-19, 21, 31-33, 37-39, 43-44, 49-51, 59

techniques, 5, 8, 18-21, 24-25, 27, 29, 57
technology, 7
temperature, 13, 15-21, 27, 32-33, 38-39, 44-47, 50-51, 53, 55
texture, 11-12, 16, 18-21, 25, 40, 4, 53
thermometers, 16, 37, 39
tomato paste, 13, 49-50, 52
tongs, 37-39, 49-50
towels, 15, 22, 25, 49-50, 55
training, 5, 57

vegetables, 5, 7-8, 11-13, 15-16, 18-21, 23-25, 27, 31-35, 37, 3, 43-44, 46-47, 49-53, 55
vinegar, 13, 19, 37-38, 43, 45, 47, 49-50

water, 11, 25, 47, 49, 51, 53
whisks, 17, 31-32, 37-39, 41, 43, 45, 47

64